MORE SONGS OF THE CHRISTMAS STORY

TRADITIONAL CAROLS THAT TELL THE TRUE STORY OF JESUS' BIRTH

Loveland, Colorado
group.com

Group
Real. **Bold.** Love.

Group resources really work!

This Group resource incorporates our R.E.A.L. approach to ministry. It reinforces a growing friendship with Jesus, encourages long-term learning, and results in life transformation, because it's:

Relational—Learner-to-learner interaction enhances learning and builds Christian friendships.

Experiential—What learners experience through discussion and action sticks with them up to 9 times longer than what they simply hear or read.

Applicable—The aim of Christian education is to equip learners to be both hearers and doers of God's Word.

Learner-based—Learners understand and retain more when the learning process takes into consideration how they learn best.

MORE Songs of the Christmas Story:
Traditional Carols That Tell the True Story of Jesus' Birth

Copyright © 2018 Group Publishing, Inc.

Visit our website: **group.com**

MORE Songs of the Christmas Story was created by the amazing and talented team at Group.

Credits
Editor: Charity Kauffman
Executive Editor: Jody Brolsma
Assistant Editors: Lyndsay Gerwing and Becky Helzer
Chief Creative Officer: Joani Schultz
Art Director: Veronica Preston
Production Designer: Mollie Bickert
Music by Dave and Jess Ray from Doorpost Songs Family Worship.

ISBN 978-1-4707-5541-6

Printed in the U.S.A.

10 9 8 7 6 5 4 3 2 1   20 19 18

TABLE OF CONTENTS

INTRODUCTION

What's one thing all sacred Christmas songs have in common? They're about Jesus! Together, their catchy melodies and well-known lyrics celebrate a baby's birth so long ago. But what child *is* this? Over the next four weeks, kids will answer that question and dig deep into what makes baby Jesus so special.

Each lesson weaves together Scripture, biblical context, hands-on experiences, discussion, history, and beloved Christmas songs. There's a little something for everyone! We've kept supplies simple so you can spend time building friendships with kids instead of prepping supplies.

And we're so excited for you to hear and sing along with four *brand-new* Christmas carol arrangements. Having heard their stories, you'll sing them in a whole new way—with your voice *and* your heart! They're available on the DVD that's included with this book. You can also use the digital access code to download the video and audio versions. Remember that these songs are copyrighted and for classroom use only. Please don't make copies to share with others.

You'll see that handouts and take-home pages *are* free to copy. You'll need them for some of the experiences and to share the songs of Christmas with families at home.

Here's an overview of what kids will discover:

WEEK	BIBLE POINT	BIBLE STORY	SONG
1	Jesus is God's Son.	An Angel Visits Mary (Luke 1:26-56)	"What Child Is This?"
2	Jesus is good news.	Jesus Is Born (Luke 2:1-20)	"Go, Tell It on the Mountain"
3	Jesus is the promised Rescuer.	Magi Travel to Bethlehem (Matthew 2:2-12)	"O Little Town of Bethlehem"
4	Jesus is the light of the world.	Simeon Sees Jesus (Luke 2:21-40)	"Hark! the Herald Angels Sing"

WHAT CHILD IS THIS?

BIBLE POINT:

Jesus is God's Son.

KEY SCRIPTURE:

An Angel Visits Mary
(Luke 1:26-56)

FOR LEADERS

Think about parents who are expecting a baby. They research, discuss, argue about (uh-oh!), and eventually land on the perfect name for their little one. Mary, however, didn't get to name her first child because *God* did it for her. God gave Jesus a perfect, if not unique, name. There may have been other babies named Jesus in Bethlehem—so what child was this? What made Jesus special? <u>Jesus is God's Son</u>. This baby was Christ the King. This baby would be the son of Mary, but also, extraordinarily, the Son of God.

When kids meet new babies in their families, they're introduced with their names: "Hayden, meet Lily." This lesson will help kids see that the baby we celebrate at Christmas wasn't just another newborn. Jesus is special because he's God's Son who came to save us. We all need salvation, so we all need to befriend this special baby.

God gave Mary a big responsibility, and Mary responded to her surprising assignment with trust and worship. God's giving you an assignment, too—to tell the kids in your group about his Son, Jesus. Trust that he'll be with you and that the Holy Spirit will overshadow you and help you. As you prepare, read Mary's song in Luke 1:46-55 as your own prayer to God, and thank him for the great things he's done in your life.

OVERVIEW

EXPERIENCES		ACTIVITIES	SUPPLIES
Get Started	10 minutes	Choose reindeer names and play a name game.	• "What Child Is This?" audio • music player
Bible Discovery	5 minutes	**Special Delivery**—Find out what the angel told Mary.	• Bibles
	10 minutes	**Impossible Is Possible**—Read a message and do a seemingly impossible task.	• Bibles • 8½x11-inch sheets of paper (1 for every 2 kids) • "Impossible Possible" handouts (1 for every 2 kids, plus extras) • child-safe scissors
	10 minutes	**Jehovah Is Salvation**—Find out what Jesus' name means.	• Bibles • whiteboard or flip chart • marker • candy canes (1 per child) • warm water • insulated paper cups (1 per child)
Music Video	3 minutes	Sing "What Child Is This?"	• "What Child Is This?" music video
Carol Story: "What Child Is This?"	10 minutes	Hear the story behind "What Child Is This?"	
Life Application and Prayer	10 minutes	Twist chenille wires into candy-cane hearts.	• Bibles • red and white chenille wires (1 of each color per child) • yarn or ribbon (one 8- to 10-inch piece per child)

⇨ GET STARTED

Welcome kids with music! Play and sing along with the "Hark! the Herald Angels Sing" and "Go, Tell It on the Mountain" music videos as kids gather.

Get kids talking with this icebreaker question.

Ask: **There's a popular poem that includes a lot of reindeer with silly names.** Review the reindeer names listed in the "'Twas the Night Before Christmas" poem. **If you could name a reindeer, what would you name it? Why would you choose that name?**

Say: **Choosing names is fun! We name our pets, our toys, and, of course, people! Today we'll discover a special baby's name *and* the special reason this baby was born. But first let's play a game to help us get to know everyone's name.**

Set the tone and create a fun and upbeat environment by playing "What Child Is This?" in the background during the game.

- Form groups of eight to 10 kids, and have each group stand in a circle.

- When you say "go," kids will go around the circle, each saying his or her name and a word that describes him or her personally that starts with the same letter—for example, "Joyful Julia." Then the child will fist bump the next person, signaling that it's his or her turn.

- To keep things moving, give groups only 30 seconds to get all the way around the circle. Have groups throw their hands in the air and cheer to show when they've finished.

- Play again, but this time, rather than saying his or her own name and describing word, everyone must say the name and describing word of the person to his or her left. Give groups only 25 seconds.

- On the last round, everyone must say the name of the person to his or her right. Give groups only 20 seconds.

- After the game, have kids return to their seats.

Not only do we know each other's names now, but we also know something about each person in our group. The baby Jesus' name tells us why he came to earth on the first Christmas. Jesus' name means "Jehovah is salvation" or "the Lord saves." <u>Jesus is God's Son</u>. We celebrate the day God sent his Son to earth to save us!

🔭 BIBLE DISCOVERY

SPECIAL DELIVERY

Ask: **Who gave you your name?** Share the story of how you got your name to begin the conversation.

Say: **Parents usually name their kids. Today people sometimes look through a book that's filled with names or search online to get ideas. But Mary and Joseph didn't do that.**

Open a Bible to Luke 1, and show it to the kids.

We find out who gave baby Jesus his name in Luke, chapter 1. Spoiler alert—it was an angel! The Bible says that God sent the angel Gabriel to visit Mary in her town called Nazareth. Mary wasn't married yet, but she was planning to marry a man named Joseph. The angel Gabriel said "hello" and told Mary that God really liked her and was with her.

Have kids turn to face a partner.

Using only facial expressions, show how you'd feel if an angel visited you at your house and told you surprising news. Pause to let kids react, and then have them tell their partners why they'd feel that way.

The Bible says that Mary was confused (pause to make a confused face) **and disturbed** (pause to make a disturbed face). **She was upset and didn't know how to react. Let's see what else the angel said to Mary.**

Read Luke 1:30-31.

Mary wasn't married yet, but she was going to have a baby, and his name would be Jesus. God would be the father, so <u>Jesus would be God's Son</u>. To Mary, that might have seemed impossible!

IMPOSSIBLE IS POSSIBLE

Form pairs, and give each pair a sheet of 8½x11-inch paper.

Say: **I have a message for you: "You will walk through a piece of paper." How can you make the message come true?**

Give pairs about a minute to brainstorm, and then interrupt their discussions.

Ask: **Does the message you received seem possible or impossible? Why?**

- **How is the message I said—"You will walk through a piece of paper"—like the message the angel gave to Mary?**

The angel's message seemed impossible. Not only would Mary have a baby, but the baby would also be God's Son who'd rule like a king forever. What?! Mary didn't laugh or say the angel was being ridiculous, but she did ask a question: "How can this be possible?" Would you like to ask me how walking through a piece of paper could be possible?

Invite kids' questions, and then distribute an "Impossible Possible" handout and scissors to each pair. Give the following instructions:

- Have kids fold the "Impossible Possible" handouts in half vertically (like a hot dog bun).

- Have kids start at the fold and follow the lines to cut six straight cuts across the paper.

- Have kids then start from the open edge of the paper and follow the lines to make five cuts in the opposite direction, between the original six cuts.

- Have kids cut the middle crease but not cut the top and bottom.

- Invite pairs to gently open their papers so the hole stretches open. Have partners hold their papers so the hole stretches wide without ripping. Each partner should be able to walk through the hole. Have a few extra precut papers on hand, just in case one accidentally tears.

- Collect the extra pieces of paper, and have kids give each other high-fives and then return to their seats.

I answered *your* question; now let's find out how the angel answered Mary's question.

Read Luke 1:35-38.

The baby would be God's Son because nothing is impossible with God. The angel also said that Mary's cousin Elizabeth was expecting a special baby, too. So Mary went to visit Elizabeth.

Ask: **Who do you go to talk to when something unusual or troubling happens?**

Share an example from your own life to begin the conversation. Then let kids share their own stories.

We don't know if Mary and Elizabeth had always been close friends, but the angel's message made Mary go see Elizabeth. The Bible says that Elizabeth's baby jumped for joy inside her tummy when Mary arrived. Even Elizabeth's baby knew Jesus was special! Let's see what Elizabeth said.

Read Luke 1:42-45.

Mary believed that God was doing something special inside her—really! She believed that her baby, Jesus, was God's Son. So why the name *Jesus*? Let's explore what his name says about him.

JEHOVAH IS SALVATION

Say: **Do you know anyone named Jesus today?** Pause for kids' reactions. **Back in Bible times, *Jesus* was a pretty popular name, but sometimes it was pronounced in different ways. In the Old Testament, it was pronounced "Joshua" or "Jeshua"** (Yeh-SHOO-ah). **So when Jesus was born, he might have had other friends named Jeshua, too. Let's find out some names that are popular today!**

BOBBY – II

MAGGIE – III

BEN

JULIA – II

HENRY

Have kids take turns shouting out their names and their family members' names. Write each name on a whiteboard or flip chart. When a name is repeated, make a tally mark beside that name. If you have a large group, divide into smaller groups and have one person in each smaller group record and tally names. If your group is small, ask kids to share friends' names, too. After each child has shared, tally the results to determine your group's most popular names.

There may have been other babies named Jesus, but Mary's baby was different. He would actually *do* what his name means. *Jesus* means "Jehovah is salvation." *Jehovah* is a name for God. And *salvation* means to rescue or save. So *Jesus* means "God rescues"! Jesus is God's Son, so he's the only Jesus who can live up to his name. Through Jesus, God would rescue his people! But what would he rescue them from? Let's see if candy canes can help answer that question.

Give each child a candy cane and a cup of warm water.

Once upon a time, this candy cane didn't have a red stripe. It was spotless and clean. And at one time, the people God created were new and clean. They were God's close friends, and nothing could pull them apart. But then sin entered the world. God is pure and perfect—he can't be anywhere near sin. So that's a problem when we have sin in our lives!

When we sin, we choose what we want over what God wants. Sin is like a sickness that ruins everything and hurts our friendship with God. But there's good news! God loves us so much that he had a plan to get rid of sin's mark. He sent his Son, Jesus, to take the punishment for sin. Jesus came to save people from sin.

Have kids break their candy canes in half. They can eat one half and put the other half into their cups of warm water. Have them observe what happens to the candy cane in the water. After several minutes, the red stripe will dissolve completely. As they wait, have kids notice that the same thing is happening to the red stripe when the candy canes are in their mouths.

Ask: **How is the water dissolving the red stripe like Jesus saving us from sin?**

Jesus came to make our hearts clean. He was 100 percent God, and he left heaven's awesomeness to be with us and get rid of sin's stain on our lives. But Jesus was also 100 percent human, so he knows what it's like to make friends, live with a family, and have people make fun of him. He knows what it's like to be tempted to do wrong. <u>Jesus is God's Son</u>. Let's read what Gabriel said about Jesus again.

Read Luke 1:31-33.

<u>Jesus is God's Son</u>. So Mary's baby would be the King of kings, and he'd bring salvation—a forever friendship with God—to people stained by sin. That means he'd wash away our sin so we can be close to God again. Let's celebrate God's Son, Jesus, who grew up to be the King of kings who took away our sin.

Collect water cups, and invite kids to enjoy the rest of their candy canes.

🎵 MUSIC VIDEO

Play the "What Child Is This?" music video, and encourage kids to sing along and do the motions. They'll really have a blast if you lead the way!

📖 CAROL STORY: "WHAT CHILD IS THIS?"

Say: **The angel's message came true! Jesus was born in Bethlehem. Just imagine what it would've been like to be there that day and hear about a baby sleeping in a manger. We might ask, "What child *is* this?"**

THE KING OF KINGS
SALVATION BRINGS

A man named William Chatterton Dix asked that question in a poem he wrote about 150 years ago. William didn't work as a poet or a musician. Instead, he sold ship insurance in Scotland. But then William got sick. He was so sick that he had to stay in bed for a long time.

Ask: **What do you do when you're sick and have to stay home?** Share an example from your own life to begin, and then let kids share.

Being sick is no fun, but that hard time brought William closer to God. God saved him from his sickness and inspired him to write a poem called "The Manger Throne." Years later, people sang William's words to a well-known tune called "Greensleeves." And we just sang the song today! What child is this? <u>Jesus is God's Son</u>!

🙏 LIFE APPLICATION AND PRAYER

Have kids sit in a circle.

Say: **William Chatterton Dix isn't the only one who wrote a song. Mary did, too! Listen to Mary's song.**

Read Luke 1:46-55.

Let's use Mary's song as a guide to help us talk to God. Close your eyes, and I'll help you know what to say.

First Mary praised God. She said, "Oh, how my soul praises the Lord!" Your soul is sort of like your heart and mind. Let's think of something God has done for us and silently tell him how great he is. Share a few examples from your own life to help get kids thinking.

Pause while kids think of something. Then invite everyone to respond, "We praise you, God."

Then Mary said what God is like—that he's mighty and holy. Let's each silently think of a word that says what God is like.

Pause while kids think. Then say, "God, you are…" and have kids say their words together.

Mary's song says how God helped people. Think about a time God helped you or someone you know. Share an example from your own life to get kids thinking.

Pause while kids think. Then have everyone say, "Thank you, God. Amen."

Today we sang these words: "The King of kings salvation brings. Let loving hearts enthrone him." There's not actually a chair inside your heart, but Jesus *can* live in us and love through us. Let's make ornaments that will remind us of the salvation and love Jesus brings.

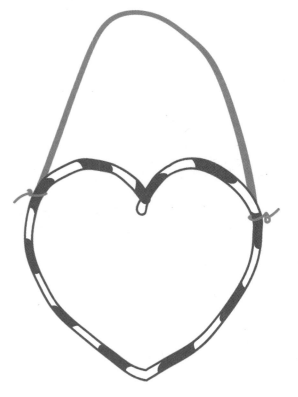

- Give each child a red chenille wire and a white chenille wire.

- Show kids how to twist a red wire and a white wire together and then shape it into a heart.

- Tie yarn or ribbon to the top of the heart to hang it.

If time remains, keep singing! We recommend "Go, Tell It on the Mountain" or "O Little Town of Bethlehem."

 # TAKE IT HOME

Distribute the take-home page for this lesson to each child, or email the page to families.

IMPOSSIBLE POSSIBLE

_____   _____

_____   _____

_____   _____

_____   _____

_____   _____

_____   _____

TAKE IT HOME
"WHAT CHILD IS THIS?"

DISCOVER

Jesus is God's Son.

READ

Luke 1:26-56

Think about parents who are expecting a baby. They research, discuss, argue about (uh-oh!), and eventually land on the perfect name for their little one. Mary, however, didn't get to name her first child because *God* did it for her. Jesus' name was perfect, if not unique. There may have been other babies named Jesus in Bethlehem—so what child was this? What made Jesus special? Jesus is God's Son. This baby was Christ the King. This baby would be the son of Mary, but also, extraordinarily, the Son of God.

SHARE

As a family, look through a book or website with baby names and meanings. Find each family member's name, and read what it means. Talk about how that person lives out his or her name.

PRAY

Have a family member read verses from Mary's song in Luke 1:49-51a. Then thank God for sending his Son, Jesus, to save us from sin so we can be close friends with God.

LISTEN

Notice when you hear the song "What Child Is This?" this week. It may be on your car radio or music you hear in stores or on TV. You can even keep track of how many times you hear it!

What child is this, who laid to rest,
On Mary's lap is sleeping?
Whom angels greet with anthems sweet,
While shepherds watch are keeping?

This, this is Christ the King,
Whom shepherds guard and angels sing.
Haste, haste to bring him laud,
The babe, the son of Mary.

So bring him incense, gold, and myrrh,
Come, peasant, king to own him;
The King of kings salvation brings.
Let loving hearts enthrone him.

This, this is Christ the King,
Whom shepherds guard and angels sing:
Haste, haste to bring him laud,
The babe, the son of Mary.

This, this is Christ the King,
Whom shepherds guard and angels sing.
Haste, haste to bring him laud,
The babe, the son of Mary.

"What Child Is This?" by William C. Dix.

WEEK TWO:
GO, TELL IT ON THE MOUNTAIN

BIBLE POINT:
Jesus is good news.

KEY SCRIPTURE:
Jesus Is Born
(Luke 2:1-20)

FOR LEADERS

Bad news is now just a click or call away. Our world seems so weighed down by sin and fear. Is there hope? Perhaps that's how people felt during the time Jesus was born. "Rome wants to tax us more?" Bad news. "We need to travel to our hometowns?" *Sigh.* "There's no place to stay?" More bad news. People needed some good news, and so do we. We need Jesus. Jesus is good news.

Kids need Jesus, too. They may not read every headline or faithfully watch the evening news, but they do feel the effects of our scary world. Sometimes the bad news does hit close to home and kids learn that grandparents are sick, parents are getting a divorce, or they've failed a test at school. This lesson will help kids discover how friendship with Jesus can bring good news to bad times, and it'll give *you* an opportunity to tell kids the good news about your own friendship with Jesus!

As you prepare, consider the angel's message to the shepherds in Luke 2:10-14, and thank God for sending Jesus—our good news of great joy!

OVERVIEW

EXPERIENCES		ACTIVITIES	SUPPLIES
Get Started	10 minutes	Talk about Christmastime travels and play a talking game.	• index cards (1 per child) • markers or pencils • timer
Bible Discovery	15 minutes	**The Christmas Story—**Use emojis to retell the Christmas story in Luke 2.	• Bibles • "Christmas Emojis" handouts (1 for every 4 kids) • poster board (1 sheet for every 4 kids) • markers or pencils • tape • child-safe scissors
	10 minutes	**Good News of Great Joy—**Use ornaments to explain how Jesus saves us from sin that weighs us down.	• small plant or Christmas tree with weak branches • 5 heavy ornaments
Music Video	3 minutes	Sing "Go, Tell It on the Mountain."	• "Go, Tell It on the Mountain" music video
Carol Story: "Go, Tell It on the Mountain"	5 minutes	Hear the story behind "Go, Tell It on the Mountain."	
Life Application and Prayer	15 minutes	Make a prayer ornament and pray for friends who need Jesus.	• large, clear plastic ball ornaments (1 per child) • small strips of red and green paper (10 per child) • markers or pens

 # GET STARTED

Welcome kids with music! Play and sing along with the "What Child Is This?" and "O Little Town of Bethlehem" music videos as kids gather.

Get kids talking with this icebreaker question.

Ask: **Where do you travel at Christmastime? Or who travels to you?** Share an example from your own life to begin.

Say: **Mary and Joseph had some traveling to do on the very first Christmas. But it wasn't their own choice. The king, Caesar Augustus, said they had to go to their hometown to be counted in a census. Being forced to travel when Mary was almost ready to have a baby may have seemed like bad news. But God was at work, getting ready to change the world forever! <u>Jesus is good news</u>. His birth is something to celebrate and talk about! Speaking of talking, let's play a game where you'll have to describe a word.**

- Give each child an index card, and have him or her write a word that has to do with Christmas. Examples include *tree, wreath, candy cane, presents,* and *stockings.* Be ready to help younger kids with spelling. If you have a smaller group, have each child make two or three cards so the game lasts longer.

- Form a circle, and number off by twos to create a "Team One" and a "Team Two."

- Gather the cards into a pile, and set them facedown in the middle of the circle. You'll use them to play the following game, which is a little like Catch Phrase or Taboo.

- Set a timer for one minute.

- When you say "go," the first Team One player will draw a card from the top of the pile and describe the word without saying the word itself. When his or her teammates guess the correct word, the first player on Team Two will draw the next card to describe for his or her team.

- The team that's *not* describing a word when the timer goes off gets a point.

- Continue playing until everyone has had a chance to describe a word. If time allows, shuffle the cards and play again. Having heard all the words once, kids may guess the words more quickly the second time around.

Ask: **What was it like to describe a word to others?**

When Jesus was born, shepherds heard the good news first, and then they told other people the good news. In their excitement, they might not have known how to explain what happened or describe the baby they'd found in a manger. But they were happy! They eagerly told people that <u>Jesus is good news</u>. Let's read about what they saw and heard.

🔭 BIBLE DISCOVERY

THE CHRISTMAS STORY

Say: Back when Jesus was born, there were no text messages, YouTube channels, or social media posts. People had to go and tell news to others. But as we read the Christmas story from Luke, chapter 2, let's imagine that we're back in time with a smartphone or tablet and we're using emojis to tell people the story of how Jesus was born.

- Form groups of three or four, and give each group a "Christmas Emojis" handout, a sheet of poster board, scissors, and tape.

- Have kids cut out each picture and use a marker or pencil to divide their poster board into four rows or sections.

- Read each section of Luke 2 on the next page, and then pause for groups to work together to retell the story with emojis. Tell kids that they can use only five emojis for each section of the story.

- Allow kids to interpret the pictures and use their creativity. There isn't one correct way to retell the story, but we've illustrated what each part of the story could look like.

Read Luke 2:1-5. Encourage kids to recap what you've read using five emojis. Give them two minutes to choose.

Read Luke 2:6-7. Encourage kids to recap what you've read using five emojis. Give them two minutes to choose.

Read Luke 2:8-14. Encourage kids to recap what you've read using five emojis. Give them two minutes to choose.

Read Luke 2:15-20. Encourage kids to recap what you've read using five emojis. Give them two minutes to choose.

Have groups pair up with another group and use their emoji boards to retell the story to each other. If you have a small class, you could have groups take turns retelling the story to the whole group. It's a story that bears repeating!

You all just told good news of great joy—Jesus is born! Let's think back to some of the details.

Ask: **As you told the story, what parts seemed like bad news at first? Why?**

- **What parts of the Christmas story are good news? Why?**

The angels brought the shepherds "good news of great joy." A Savior or Rescuer had been born. Let's explore why Jesus' birth was such good news.

GOOD NEWS OF GREAT JOY

Say: **First we have to understand the bad news.**

Place a small plant or Christmas tree (think Charlie Brown tree) in front of the kids, along with five heavy ornaments.

Watch what happens when I put these heavy ornaments on our little tree. These ornaments are pretty. They remind me that sometimes sin can seem good or fun. For example, watching that not-so-good movie seems fun, or teasing a kid at school seems cool, or telling a little lie might seem to keep you out of trouble. But sin weighs us down and ruins everything.

Hang a heavy ornament on a branch, causing the branch to bend with the weight.

We can read about how sin hurt God's people in the Old Testament of the Bible. Sin ruined God's friendship with his people, the Israelites.

God's people walked away from God and his rules time and time again.

Place another heavy ornament on the tree.

Because of their sin, God's people lost everything—their land, their king, and their hope for a good future.

Place another heavy ornament on the tree.

Sin messes up our lives, too. It can hurt our friendships with other people. Sin makes people argue and fight.

Place another heavy ornament on the tree.

Sin makes us behave selfishly and put what we want in front of what other people need.

Place another heavy ornament on the tree.

Ask: **Describe what the ornaments are doing to the tree.**

- **What do you imagine will happen to the tree if we leave all these heavy things on it for a long time?**

- **How do the tree and ornaments remind you of what sin does to us?**

Sin is bad news. Sin hurts us and separates us from God. We need a Rescuer to bring salvation and save us from sin. We need Jesus! <u>Jesus is good news</u> because through him, God took away the weight and burden of sin. Because Jesus is God's Son, he's more powerful than sin. He beat sin once and for all when he died on the cross.

Jesus is good news because he forgives our sin.

Remove an ornament from the tree.

Jesus is good news because sin can't take away his love for us.

Remove an ornament from the tree.

Jesus is good news because he's always with us. Sin can't separate us from God anymore.

Remove an ornament from the tree.

Jesus is good news because he helps us when we're tempted to sin.

Remove an ornament from the tree.

And **Jesus is good news** because his love is for everyone! So like the shepherds, we can go and tell everyone about salvation through Jesus!

Remove the last ornament from the tree.

Let me tell *you* about how *I* met Jesus! Take this opportunity to tell the kids in your class about how your own friendship with Jesus started. Tell about a time you asked Jesus to forgive your sin and be your forever friend.

Let's retell the story of Christmas one more time—this time through music!

MUSIC VIDEO

Play the "Go, Tell It on the Mountain" music video, and encourage kids to sing along and do the motions. They'll really have a blast if you lead the way!

AND GOD SENT US **SALVATION** THAT BLESSED CHRISTMAS MORN!

CAROL STORY: "GO, TELL IT ON THE MOUNTAIN"

Say: **The chorus is so catchy! And it's been sung for a *long* time. "Go, Tell It on the Mountain" is an African-American spiritual that was sung by slaves in the United States. After slavery ended, people still knew and sang the chorus, but it wasn't written down anywhere. Then about a hundred years ago, John Wesley Work Jr. wrote new verses and included the song in a songbook.**

John Wesley Work Jr. was the choir director at Fisk University, a college that was started for former slaves. His choir was called the Fisk Jubilee Singers, and they traveled around the country to raise money for their school. Some people weren't sure if an African-American spiritual like "Go, Tell It on the Mountain" should be sung because it came from a bad time when people were hurt and mistreated. But John wanted to sing songs like these because they bring good news of great joy even during bad times.

Ask: **Tell about a time in your life God turned something bad into something good.** Share an example from your own life to begin. Perhaps you lost a job but then found a new and better one. Or maybe moving to a new home led to meeting and making new friends.

Spirituals like "Go, Tell It on the Mountain" celebrate that even in bad times, <u>Jesus is good news</u>. He brings salvation when we need it the most.

LIFE APPLICATION AND PRAYER

Say: **The angels invited the shepherds to meet Jesus, and after they met him, the shepherds spread the news so others could hear about him, too.**

Ask: **Who's someone you know who needs Jesus?** Share an example from your own life to begin. It could be someone who knows Jesus but is going through a hard time or someone who has never met Jesus before.

Let's make ornaments for our Christmas trees at home. This ornament won't weigh the tree down but will lift people up in prayer!

- Give each child at least 10 strips of red and green paper. Have kids write on their strips names of people they know who need Jesus.

- Give each child a large, clear plastic ball ornament, and have kids remove the tops so they can place the rolled-up strips inside.

- Show kids how to roll the strips tightly and then drop them into the ornament. It's okay if the strips unroll a bit inside the ornament—it'll fill the ball with color!

- Secure the top again so the ornament is ready to hang.

Every time you see this ornament on your tree, remember to pray for the people whose names are inside. <u>Jesus is good news</u>, and he'll work in amazing ways to help and bring hope to the people we love.

If time remains, keep singing! We recommend "What Child Is This?" or "Hark! the Herald Angels Sing."

 # TAKE IT HOME

Distribute the take-home page for this lesson to each child, or email the page to families.

CHRISTMAS EMOJIS

 MORE SONGS OF THE CHRISTMAS STORY

 TAKE IT HOME
"GO, TELL IT ON THE MOUNTAIN"

DISCOVER

Jesus is good news.

READ

Luke 2:1-20

Bad news is now just a click or call away. Our world seems so weighed down by sin and fear. Is there hope? Perhaps that's how people felt during the time Jesus was born. "Rome wants to tax us more?" Bad news. "We need to travel to our hometowns?" *Sigh.* "There's no place to stay?" More bad news. People needed some good news, and so do we. We need Jesus. Jesus is good news. Jesus shows us how much God loves us. God sent us salvation through Jesus. That's good news!

SHARE

Parents, take this opportunity to tell your kids about how your own friendship with Jesus started. Tell about a time you asked Jesus to forgive your sin and be your forever friend.

PRAY

Find a heavier ornament on your Christmas tree, and place it on one of the bottom branches so it hangs lower than the tree. Gather around the tree, and pray. First silently talk to God about sin in your life; then pray out loud and thank God that when we were weighed down with sin, he sent Jesus to save us from sin and bring us close to God again. Give a group hug, and then put the ornament on a sturdy branch again.

LISTEN

Notice when you hear the song "Go, Tell It on the Mountain" this week. It may be on your car radio or music you hear in stores or on TV. You can even keep track of how many times you hear it!

 Group
Real. Bold. Love.

SONG LYRICS
"GO, TELL IT ON THE MOUNTAIN"

Chorus:
Go, tell it on the mountain,
Over the hills and everywhere.
Go, tell it on the mountain
That Jesus Christ is born.

While shepherds kept their watching
O'er silent flocks by night,
Behold, throughout the heavens
There shone a holy light.
(Chorus)

The shepherds feared and trembled
When lo, above the earth,
Rang out the angel chorus
That hailed our Savior's birth.
(Chorus)

Down in a lowly manger
The humble Christ was born.
And God sent us salvation
That blessed Christmas morn.
(Chorus)

Go, tell it on the mountain!

"Go, Tell It on the Mountain" by John W. Work, Jr.

O LITTLE TOWN OF BETHLEHEM

BIBLE POINT:
Jesus is the promised Rescuer.

KEY SCRIPTURE:
Magi Travel to Bethlehem (Matthew 2:1-12)

FOR LEADERS

"A promise made is a promise kept." Does this adage hold true in your life? Especially at Christmas, we may find ourselves making promises without thinking things through. "You can have an extra cookie if you wear your nice Christmas outfit to church." "I can host Christmas at my house." "I promise not to spend too much money." Even though we sometimes break our promises, God always keeps his promises. When God promised to help his people in the Old Testament, he was already thinking of Jesus' birth in Bethlehem. Jesus is the promised Rescuer. Jesus' birth brings us hope and calms our fears.

Kids keep track of promises, don't they? They remember when they're owed a piece of candy, and if you tell them you'll play in five minutes, they'll be ready and waiting when the second hand strikes. But as they get older, kids realize that people don't always keep their promises. Assure kids that in Jesus, they have a friend who will never let them down. Jesus will "cast out sin and enter in" to their lives and hearts today.

Long before Jesus was born, prophets promised God's people that a Messiah, or Rescuer, would come. As you prepare this lesson, read some of those promises, and thank God for his plan to send Jesus. Check out Micah 5:2; Isaiah 7:14; and Isaiah 9:6-7.

OVERVIEW

EXPERIENCES		ACTIVITIES	SUPPLIES
Get Started	5 minutes	Talk about promises people have made.	
Bible Discovery	10 minutes	**Broken Promises**—See how water brings "hope" to broken toothpicks.	• toothpicks (5 per child) • disposable plastic plates (1 per child) • drinking straws (1 per child) • water • cups (several for each table)
	15 minutes	**Magi Mystery**—Search for stars that tell about the magis' journey to Bethlehem.	• Bibles • signs that say "Jerusalem," "Temple," "Palace," and "Bethlehem" • 4 sheets of paper, each cut into a star shape
	5 minutes	**Hopes and Fears**—Fill up a stocking with hopes and fears.	• red and green paper wads • Christmas stocking
Music Video	3 minutes	Sing "O Little Town of Bethlehem."	• "O Little Town of Bethlehem" music video
Carol Story: "O Little Town of Bethlehem"	15 minutes	Hear the story behind "O Little Town of Bethlehem" and create new Christmas songs.	• paper • pencils (1 for every 2 kids)
Life Application and Prayer	5 minutes	Pray three of God's promises.	

⇨ GET STARTED

Welcome kids with music! Play and sing along with the "What Child Is This?" and "Go, Tell It on the Mountain" music videos as kids gather.

Get kids talking with this icebreaker question.

Ask: **Tell about a promise someone made to you. What was it? Did the person keep it?** Tell a story from your own life to begin. Perhaps your parents promised to stop for ice cream after a grocery shopping trip or traveling family members promised to text you to let you know that they arrived safely.

Say: **Waaaaay back in the Bible—a long time before Jesus was born—people called *prophets* spoke messages from God. Even though God's people, the Israelites, had gotten themselves into trouble because of their sin, prophets told them that God would send a Rescuer to help them. They waited year after year, but a Rescuer never came. Maybe they thought God had broken his promise. But many years later something out-of-the-ordinary happened. Magi, or scholars, from a different land saw a new star in the sky, and God fulfilled his promise! He hadn't broken it! Let's do an experiment to see how water can change something that's broken.**

👓 BIBLE DISCOVERY

BROKEN PROMISES

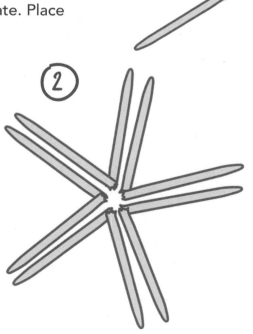

- Give each child five toothpicks, a straw, and a plate. Place several cups of water within reach.

- Have kids break each toothpick in half, but not all the way (1). Have extra toothpicks on hand to replace those that may break completely.

- Show kids how to lay the toothpicks on the plate so the broken edges almost touch in the middle (2).

Say: **These toothpicks look broken and useless. But watch what happens when we add some water to the center of our plates.**

- Have kids use straws to draw water from the cups.

- Have kids slowly drop the water from the straws into the middle of the toothpicks and watch what happens (3). The toothpicks will move into a star shape! Kids may need to coax the star a bit by dropping water on and around each point that takes shape. If too much water escapes and "drowns" the star, have kids remove the water from the plate and try again.

When promises are broken, we feel disappointed and let down. Perhaps that's how God's people felt before Jesus was born. God's promises may have seemed like a useless pile of toothpicks.

Ask: **How did the water change the broken toothpicks?**

The water helped move the toothpicks into place and, with a little nudging, created something beautiful—a star! God put his rescue plan in motion when he sent Jesus to earth as a baby that first Christmas. <u>Jesus is the promised Rescuer</u>. His birth proves that God keeps his promises. God used a star in the sky to announce this special baby's birth, and the magi were the first to see it. Let's find out more about these stargazers' journey to Bethlehem.

MAGI MYSTERY

Ahead of time, hang a location sign in each corner of your space. You'll need a sign for each of these locations: Jerusalem, Temple, Palace, and Bethlehem. Then write the following verse references on stars. There are four verses, so you'll have a total of four stars.

- Star 1 (Jerusalem)—Matthew 2:1-3

- Star 2 (Temple)—Matthew 2:6; Micah 5:2

- Star 3 (Palace)—Matthew 2:8

- Star 4 (Bethlehem)—Matthew 2:9-11

Hide each star in the corresponding area of your room for kids to find. Be creative! The magis' journey wasn't easy, either!

Say: **In the book of Matthew, the Bible mentions magi. People think the magi were** probably from the land of Persia, which was east of Jerusalem and Bethlehem. And you *may* have heard people sing popular Christmas songs that say they were kings… but they probably weren't. Instead, they were wise men who studied the stars in the sky *and* the Old Testament Scriptures. A new star in the sky reminded them about the promised Messiah, or Rescuer, who'd be born in Bethlehem.

Let's imagine that we're magi on a journey to find Jesus, the promised Rescuer. Have kids stand, and guide them through pretending to pack a bag, saddle a camel, and then get in a long line like a caravan. **We'll travel together around our room and search for a star in each area. The star will point us to a verse to read in Matthew, chapter 2.**

Have all the kids move with you to the Jerusalem corner. Feel free to add some fun by circling the room several times and singing a silly version of "Sally the Camel" as you walk together. Eventually stop near the Jerusalem sign, and have kids find the star you've hidden there. Give clues to help if needed. Once the star is found, ask for a willing child to look up and read the verse on the back of the star, Matthew 2:1-3.

Ask: **Why do you think Herod—and the other people—were disturbed by the magis' question?**

The magi had studied the stars and the Old Testament *a lot*. They had read God's promises, so they were looking for the new king of the Jews. Herod didn't like that idea—a new king? *He* was the king! So he wanted to talk to people who worked at the Temple in Jerusalem. Surely they would know what these wise guys were talking about! Let's journey to the Temple and see what they said.

Have all the kids move with you in a caravan to the "Temple" corner of the room and look for the star. Once it's found, ask a willing child to read Matthew 2:6 and another willing child to read Micah 5:2.

These two verses say the same thing, but one was spoken by a prophet named Micah a long, long, looooong time before Jesus was born! The other one comes from the book of Matthew in the New Testament. The people who worked at the Temple said God had promised that a ruler would come from Bethlehem.

Ask: **How might Herod have felt to hear that people were hoping for another king?**

Herod was not happy. So the Bible says he asked the magi to meet him in the palace. Let's go there and look for another star.

Have all the kids move with you in a caravan to the "Palace" corner of the room and find the star. Once it's found, ask a willing child to look up and read Matthew 2:8.

Herod wanted the magi to go to Bethlehem and then come back and give him the inside scoop. So off they went to Bethlehem! Let's go!

Have all the kids move with you in a caravan to the "Bethlehem" corner of the room and find the star. Once the star is found, ask a willing child to look up and read Matthew 2:9-11.

The magi were filled with great joy when they found Jesus. They gave him special gifts: gold, frankincense, and myrrh.

Ask: **When have you been filled with great joy? What did that feel like?** Share a story from your own life to begin the conversation.

There's usually a reason for great joy. For example, our team won a game, we unwrapped the present we've been hoping for, or we're having our favorite food for dinner! The magi were happy because the promise they'd read about happened right before their eyes. <u>Jesus is the promised Rescuer.</u> He was just a little baby, but he was God's plan to rescue people.

Point toward the "Palace" corner. **After the magi saw Jesus and gave him gifts, they did not go back to tell Herod. God had warned them in a dream to avoid going back, so they went home another way.** Lead kids the opposite direction back to their seats.

HOPES AND FEARS

Say: **The little town of Bethlehem became an important place! Micah had talked about it, Mary and Joseph traveled there, the shepherds walked its streets talking about a baby's birth, and then later some super-smart people followed a star to this little village. All these events weren't a coincidence. They were part of a promise kept. People had hoped a Rescuer would come, and they feared he never would. But there in Bethlehem, Jesus came.**

Ask: **What fears do you think the magi might have had during their journey?**

Our lives are filled with hopes and fears, too. Turn to a partner and finish this sentence: "This Christmas, I hope to get _____." Pause to let partners tell each other their Christmas hopes. **Now let's take turns calling out the hopes you shared. I'll add a red paper wad to this stocking for each hope you share.** Start at one side of the room and ask for each child's hope. With each hope, add a red paper wad to the stocking.

We also have fears. Fears often show up in our lives as "what ifs." Add a green paper wad for each fear mentioned. **What if we don't have enough money to give presents this year? What if family members get into fights when we're all together? What if someone I love gets sick and Christmas is sad? What if people don't like me?**

Ask: **What other fears do we have sometimes?** As kids answer, keep adding paper wads until the stocking is full.

Like people filled up Bethlehem, hopes and fears filled up this stocking. But even though there are hopes and fears in our hearts, there's always room for Jesus, too. Our friend Jesus is always with us. He's Immanuel, which means "God with us." We can invite Jesus to come to our hearts, and he'll give us hope and calm our fears, no matter what we're going through. Let's sing about that now.

♫ MUSIC VIDEO

Play the "O Little Town of Bethlehem" music video, and encourage kids to sing along and do the motions. It'll be extra meaningful if you lead the way!

📖 CAROL STORY: "O LITTLE TOWN OF BETHLEHEM"

Ask: **If you could go on a journey to anywhere in the world, where would you go?** Share your own answer to begin.

Say: **Many years ago, a man named Phillips Brooks was a pastor at a church in Philadelphia. One December, Phillips got to go on the trip of a lifetime. He went to Israel, where Jesus lived a long time ago. There were no airplanes, so he had to travel by boat. On Christmas Eve, he rode on horseback down the same path that the magi took from Jerusalem to Bethlehem. What an unforgettable journey!**

THE HOPES AND FEARS OF ALL THE YEARS ARE MET IN THEE TONIGHT.

Several years later, Phillips was making plans for his church's Sunday school Christmas program. His fond memories of Bethlehem inspired him to write a poem. He asked his musician friend Lewis Redner to put it to music so everyone could sing it at the Christmas program.

Lewis agreed and promised to write the music. But try as he might, he just couldn't come up with a melody. Even on the night before the program, it looked like Lewis wouldn't be able to keep his promise. But then while trying to sleep, a melody popped into his head! He got up, wrote it down, and added Phillips' poem. It was perfect! Lewis kept his promise, and people sang "O Little Town of Bethlehem" the next day. And we just sang it today, too! Phillips and Lewis wrote the song together. Let's see if you can work with a friend to write new words for a Christmas tune.

Form pairs, and give each pair paper and a pencil. Have one partner write two sentences about Christmas—even better if the sentences rhyme! Then have the second partner sing the words to a common Christmas tune. It could be a song like "Jingle Bells" or "We Wish You a Merry Christmas." Ask for willing kids to perform their new songs for the group.

LIFE APPLICATION AND PRAYER

Say: **<u>Jesus is the promised Rescuer</u>. Because Jesus makes us friends with God, we can hold on to God's promises when we journey through hard things in life.**

Invite kids to pray with you as you read and thank God for three of his promises.

"Don't be afraid, for I am with you. Don't be discouraged, for I am your God. I will strengthen you and help you. I will hold you up with my victorious right hand" (Isaiah 41:10).

In response, have kids say the following with you: **Thank you, God, for keeping your promises.**

"This is my command—be strong and courageous! Do not be afraid or discouraged. For the Lord your God is with you wherever you go" (Joshua 1:9).

In response, have kids say the following with you: **Thank you, God, for keeping your promises.**

"And be sure of this: I am with you always, even to the end of the age" (Matthew 28:20).

In response, have kids say the following with you: **Thank you, God, for keeping your promises.**

Thank you, Jesus. We love you. Amen.

If time remains, keep singing! We recommend "What Child Is This?" or "Hark! the Herald Angels Sing."

 TAKE IT HOME

Distribute the take-home page for this lesson to each child, or email the page to families.

TAKE IT HOME
"O LITTLE TOWN OF BETHLEHEM"

DISCOVER

Jesus is the promised Rescuer.

READ

Matthew 2:1-12

"A promise made is a promise kept." Does this adage hold true in your family's life? Especially at Christmas, we may find ourselves making promises without thinking things through. "You can have an extra cookie if you wear your nice Christmas outfit to church." "I can host Christmas at my house." "I promise not to spend too much money." Even though we sometimes break our promises, God always keeps his promises. When God promised to help his people in the Old Testament, he was already thinking of Jesus' birth in a village called Bethlehem. Jesus is the promised Rescuer. Jesus' birth brings us hope and calms our fears.

SHARE

Write each family member's name on a small piece of paper. Place the papers in a cup, and then have each person draw a name. (Family members can draw again if they get their own names.) Have each family member make a promise to the person whose name he or she drew—for example, "Mom, I promise to clean my room." Make promises…and then keep them before the week (or even day!) is over.

PRAY

Read Isaiah 41:10; Joshua 1:9; and Matthew 28:20. Then pray and thank God for ways he has kept those promises to your family.

LISTEN

Notice when you hear the song "O Little Town of Bethlehem" this week. It may be on your car radio or music you hear in stores or on TV. You can even keep track of how many times you hear it!

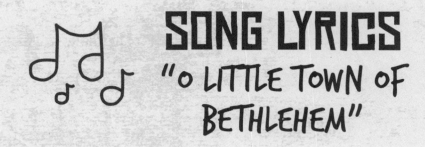

SONG LYRICS
"O LITTLE TOWN OF BETHLEHEM"

O little town of Bethlehem,
How still we see thee lie.
Above thy deep and dreamless sleep
The silent stars go by.

Yet in thy dark streets shineth
The everlasting Light.
The hopes and fears of all the years
Are met in thee tonight.

O holy Child of Bethlehem,
Descend to us, we pray.
Cast out our sin and enter in,
Be born in us today.

We hear the Christmas angels
The great glad tidings tell,
O come to us, abide with us,
Our Lord Emmanuel.

O come to us, abide with us,
Our Lord Emmanuel.

"O Little Town of Bethlehem" by Phillips Brooks.

HARK! THE HERALD ANGELS SING

BIBLE POINT:
Jesus is the light of the world.

KEY SCRIPTURE:
Simeon Sees Jesus (Luke 2:21-40)

FOR LEADERS

Have you ever lost electricity in your home for an extended amount of time? At first, living in darkness brings fun and adventure. But as minutes turn to hours and hours turn to days, it becomes increasingly difficult to prepare food, read before bed, or determine which toothbrush is yours. Imagine living in darkness for hundreds of years! The Israelites didn't actually live in the dark (although they *did* live without electricity), but they couldn't see what God was up to. They didn't notice a special baby's birth. But Simeon saw baby Jesus and recognized him right away. Jesus is the light of the world!

Maybe that's why we're drawn to Christmas lights. They bring light to the dark of winter and spark our childlike sense of wonder and imagination. Like a string of lights transforms a barren tree, Jesus shines his light to the world through kids! Have you seen it? Have you noticed the child who lets a younger friend go first? Have you heard kids pray for people in need with simple sincerity? Have you joined kids in wholeheartedly praising the newborn King?

As you prepare to share Jesus' light and life with kids this week, read Simeon's words of praise in Luke 2:29-32. Ask God to help you recognize his light shining in our world. Perhaps it's through the kids you teach! Think about and thank God for ways he's shining through their young lives.

OVERVIEW

EXPERIENCES		ACTIVITIES	SUPPLIES
Get Started	5 minutes	Talk about Christmas lights.	
Bible Discovery	10 minutes	**Christmas Light Makeovers**—Work in groups to light up parts of the room.	• classroom furniture • strings of Christmas lights (1 for every 4 kids) • extension cords (1 for every 4 kids) • "Hark! the Herald Angels Sing" audio • music player
	10 minutes	**What Babies Need**—List things that babies need.	• battery-operated candles (1 for every 8-10 kids)
	10 minutes	**Meeting Jesus**—Discover Simeon's and Anna's responses to meeting baby Jesus.	• Bibles • round striped peppermint candies (red and white or green and white) (1 per child) • small disposable white plates (1 per child) • cups of water (1 per child)
Music Video	3 minutes	Sing "Hark! the Herald Angels Sing."	• "Hark! the Herald Angels Sing" music video
Carol Story: "Hark! the Herald Angels Sing"	5 minutes	Hear the story behind "Hark! the Herald Angels Sing."	• whiteboard or large piece of paper • marker
Life Application and Prayer	15 minutes	Thank Jesus for bringing light to a dark time in life; then make a musical candle craft.	• wax paper (one 12x10-inch piece per child) • tea light (at least 1 for a sample; 1 per child if possible) • Christmas sheet music (to cut into strips) • ribbon • clear tape • child-safe scissors

 # GET STARTED

Welcome kids with music! Play and sing along with the "O Little Town of Bethlehem" and "Go, Tell It on the Mountain" music videos as kids gather.

Get kids talking with this icebreaker question.

Ask: **Tell about the best Christmas lights you've seen this year. What do you like about Christmas lights?** Give an example from what you've seen to begin the conversation.

Say: **Christmas lights shine and bring joy and fun to our neighborhoods. Jesus' birth brings light and joy to the world, too. <u>Jesus is the light of the world</u>. Through Jesus, God sent light and life to people in Bible times** *and* **to us today. Let's play a game that'll bring light and life to our room!**

 # BIBLE DISCOVERY

CHRISTMAS LIGHT MAKEOVERS

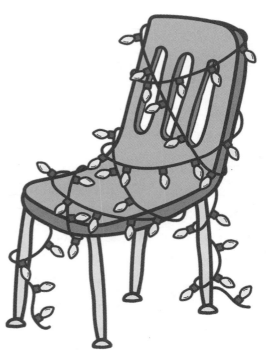

- Form groups of four, and give each group a string of Christmas lights.

- Plug in extension cords around your space, and position each group near a cord.

- Have groups choose an object in their area to decorate. It could be a chair, a table, a bookshelf, or another piece of furniture in your space.

- Play "Hark! the Herald Angels Sing." While the song plays, have kids work together in their groups to light up their objects. Tell groups that they must finish decorating by the time the song ends.

- Turn off the room lights, and travel with the kids around the room to "ooh" and "aah" at the groups' creations. Then leave the room lights off as you gather in the center of your space with only the Christmas lights illuminated.

Ask: **How did these Christmas lights change our room?**

Say: **Without these pretty lights, we'd just be sitting here in darkness. We might not like to hang out in the dark because it feels lonely, gloomy, or even spooky. On the other hand, when lights are on, we're able to see things that come our way. During the time Jesus was born, God's people may have felt like they were living in darkness. Things had gotten kind of hard for them. They didn't have their own king, their leaders treated them badly, and they missed the days of being a great nation that people looked up to. Today we'll meet two people who lived back then. Despite dark times, Simeon and Anna trusted that God would keep his promise and send a Rescuer to light up their lives. Imagine their joy when they finally met baby Jesus!** <u>**Jesus is the light of the world**</u>**. He brings light to our lives today, too.**

WHAT BABIES NEED

Say: **Let's start by thinking about what happens after a baby is born today.**

If you have a large group, you may want to break into smaller groups of eight to 10 kids. Each group will need a battery-operated candle. Hold up an illuminated candle.

Ask: **What things do babies need when they come home from the hospital? Let's answer this question together with a little game.**

Let's pretend that this candle is a baby. We'll gently pass it around our circle. The first person to hold the candle will say one thing a baby needs—for example, "A baby needs a car seat." Then he or she will pass the candle to the next person. That person will repeat what the person before said and then add something else to the list. We'll go all the way around the circle and see if we can come up with—and remember—a big list of baby stuff. Begin passing the candle around the circle. Be ready to help kids who struggle to remember what was said before.

Babies need a lot of stuff! Plus, they have to go to the doctor *and* be ready to meet grandparents, aunts, uncles, and other people who are eager to meet them. Things were a little different for baby Jesus and his parents, Mary and

Joseph. They didn't have car seats or even grandparents nearby. But they did need to travel to Jerusalem.

First Jesus needed to go to the Temple for a special ceremony where he'd officially receive his name—Jesus. Then God's law said that about a month later, parents needed to go back to the Temple to dedicate the baby and offer a sacrifice as a gift to God. When Joseph and Mary went to the Temple, they met two people who'd been waiting for God to send a Rescuer. Let's read about them.

MEETING JESUS

Read Luke 2:25-26.

Say: **We don't know much about Simeon. But we *do* know that he was God's close friend. God had told Simeon that he would get to meet God's Rescuer before he died. Imagine Simeon's joy when he met Jesus!**

Read Luke 2:27-29.

Ask: **How do you think Simeon knew that Jesus wasn't an ordinary baby?**

The Bible says that the Spirit led Simeon to the Temple. So somehow God let Simeon know that Jesus was the person he'd been waiting for. It was like God turned the lights on to reveal what Simeon was waiting to see.

Have a willing child turn your room lights on.

When Simeon held Jesus, he didn't talk baby talk or sing a silly lullaby. Instead, he praised God! He thanked God for this Rescuer who'd bring light and salvation. But he wasn't just talking about God's people, the Israelites.

Read Luke 2:30-32.

Simeon talked about Jesus saving *all* people. He said that Jesus is a light that would show many nations who God is. Jesus wasn't just the light of the Israelites. <u>Jesus is the light of the *world*</u>. Just think, Simeon praised God for sending Jesus to light up our lives, too!

A prophet named Anna got to meet baby Jesus, too. Remember, a prophet is someone who tells messages from God. Let's read about what happened when Anna met baby Jesus at the Temple.

Read Luke 2:36-38.

It sounds like Anna had gone through a dark time in her life. After her husband died, she devoted the rest of her life to worship and prayer and spent a lot of time at the Temple. She must have overheard Simeon talking to Mary and Joseph about salvation and light from God. Seeing baby Jesus brightened up her day, and she told people about this special little boy.

Ask: **Think about a time God unexpectedly brightened *your* day.** Share a story from your own life to begin the conversation; then let kids share their stories.

Sometimes unexpected surprises are fun! Let's check out a surprising experiment!

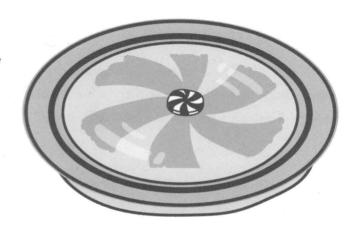

- Give each child a round striped peppermint candy. Have him or her unwrap the candy and place it in the middle of a small disposable white plate.

- Then have kids slowly pour water onto their plates so the bottoms fill up completely with water. Watch as the red or green stripes gradually spread out to the edges of the plates.

Ask: **What happened to the color in the water?**

- **How does that remind you of what Jesus' light does to our world?**

<u>**Jesus is the light of the world**</u>. He doesn't just save *you* from sin and *me* from sin, but he rescues the *whole world*! Sin in our lives leads to death and being away from God forever. But Jesus beat sin and death when he died on the cross for our sins. When we're friends with Jesus, we get to live with him forever. Like the angels brought light and life to shepherds on a hillside, Jesus brings us light and life, too. Let's sing a song to give glory to Jesus, the newborn King!

♫ MUSIC VIDEO

Play the "Hark! the Herald Angels Sing" music video, and encourage kids to sing along and do the motions. It'll be extra meaningful if you lead the way!

📖 CAROL STORY: "HARK! THE HERALD ANGELS SING"

Say: **It seems like there are two kinds of Christmas songs—songs about Jesus that we sing in church, and other songs about snow, jingle bells, and Santa that we hear on the radio or on Christmas movies. Let's make a list of both kinds of Christmas songs.**

Divide a whiteboard or large piece of paper into two columns. Invite kids to shout out names of songs for each column.

You'd think that a song like "Hark! the Herald Angels Sing" would only be on the church side. But this song brings light and life to inside *and* outside church walls.

Creating this song was a group effort. Over 300 years ago, a church leader named Charles Wesley wrote most of the words, and then later another church leader named George Whitefield changed the words a little. Meanwhile, a composer named Felix Mendelssohn had written a beautiful song to celebrate not the birth of Jesus but the anniversary of the printing press! People must have been *really* happy to not have to copy words and music by hand anymore! Felix didn't think that adding words about Jesus was good idea, but a musician named William Hayman Cummings did it anyway. He combined Charles's and George's words with Felix's music to make "Hark! the Herald Angels Sing."

This song was printed in church songbooks and sung to celebrate Jesus, the light of the world. But it's also featured in two really popular Christmas movies!

Charlie Brown and his friends sing it at the end of *A Charlie Brown Christmas*. "Hark! the Herald Angels Sing" also ends a movie called *It's a Wonderful Life*, in which all the movie characters are gathered in a living room singing "glory to the newborn King"!

Like Jesus' light shines to the whole world, today "Hark! the Herald Angels Sing" shines Jesus' light through people's TVs! This song brings light and life to the world!

 # LIFE APPLICATION AND PRAYER

Have kids close their eyes and think of dark or sad things in their lives. Perhaps people in their families are sick, they miss friends who live far away, or they're struggling to make friends at school. Invite kids to silently talk to Jesus about the darkness and ask how they can help shine Jesus' light in those situations.

Then have kids open their eyes as you close with this prayer.

Pray: **Jesus, thank you for bringing light and life to our dark times. Thanks for coming to earth so we can meet you and become your friend. Please shine your light through our lives, even after Christmas is over. We love you. Amen.**

Say: **Let's make candle shades to remind us that <u>Jesus is the light of the world</u>.**

- Ahead of time, make a sample for kids to see.

- Show kids the sample and the battery-operated tea light you've placed inside. If you don't have a tea light for each child, show kids what it looks like so they can search for one at home.

- Give each child a piece of wax paper that's approximately 12x10 inches.

- Show kids how to fold the wax paper in half horizontally, leaving about a half inch at the top.

- Have kids fold the paper in half two more times, leaving two more half inches at the top.

- Have each child roll the wax paper into a cylinder, nest one end inside the other, and then secure the circle with a piece of tape.

- Have each child choose and cut out a line of music from Christmas sheet music and then wrap the music paper around the bottom of the cylinder.

- Help kids cut and tie a piece of ribbon around the candle shade.

- Let kids take turns placing a tea light inside their shades to see how it illuminates their candle shades. Invite kids to put their candle shades somewhere that will remind them to shine Jesus' light in their lives.

If time remains, keep singing! We recommend "What Child Is This?" or "O Little Town of Bethlehem."

 TAKE IT HOME

Distribute the take-home page for this lesson to each child, or email the page to families.

DISCOVER

Jesus is the light of the world.

READ

Luke 2:21-40

Have you ever lost electricity in your home for an extended amount of time? At first, living in darkness brings fun and adventure. But as minutes turn to hours and hours turn to days, it becomes increasingly difficult to prepare food, read before bed, or determine which toothbrush is yours. Imagine living in darkness for hundreds of years! The Israelites didn't actually live in the dark (although they *did* live without electricity), but they couldn't see what God was up to. Most people couldn't see well enough to notice a special baby's birth. But Simeon saw baby Jesus and recognized him right away. Jesus is the light of the world!

SHARE

Go for a walk in your neighborhood or hop in the car to go look at Christmas lights. After the journey, have each family member choose a favorite display and tell why he or she liked it. You could even deliver Christmas candy or cookies to the homes as a way to say thank you for lighting up your Christmas season.

PRAY

Pray for Jesus to shine his light to the world through your family. Pass around a real or battery-operated candle and pray for Jesus' light to shine through each person as he or she holds the candle.

LISTEN

Notice when you hear the song "Hark! the Herald Angels Sing" this week. It may be on your car radio or music you hear in stores or on TV. You can even keep track of how many times you hear it!

SONG LYRICS
"HARK! THE HERALD ANGELS SING"

Whoa! Whoa!
Whoa! Whoa!

Hark! the herald angels sing,
"Glory to the newborn King!
Peace on earth, and mercy mild;
God and sinners reconciled."

Joyful, all ye nations rise.
Join the triumph of the skies.
With the angelic host proclaim,
"Christ is born in Bethlehem!"

Hark! the herald angels sing,
"Glory to the newborn King!"

Hail the heaven-born Prince of Peace!
Hail the Sun of Righteousness!
Light and life to all he brings,
Risen with healing in his wings.

Mild he lays his glory by,
Born that man no more may die;
Born to raise the sons of earth;
Born to give them second birth.

Hark! the herald angels sing,
"Glory to the newborn King!"

"Hark! the Herald Angels Sing" by Charles Wesley and Felix Mendelssohn.

Group
Real. Bold. Love.

WANT MORE QUICK CHILDREN'S MINISTRY LESSONS?

KIDMIN QUICK PICKS are the perfect solution!

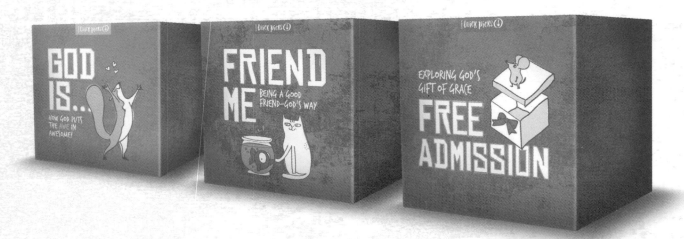

These easy-to-use, downloadable lessons are packed with interactive learning experiences, fun activities, media, and thought-provoking discussion questions that'll deepen kids' faith.

EACH VERSATILE 4-WEEK LESSON PACK INCLUDES...

4 complete, Bible-based lessons

4 Parent Pages to give parents a starting point to talk with their kids about what they learned or discovered

Teaching Video to illustrate lesson points and let kids explore faith points more deeply

Countdown Video for the start of each lesson time

Graphics Pack with lesson helps, plus publicity tools and media templates so you can spread the word about your series

- Promotional Poster (11x17)
- Editable Bulletin Insert
- 2 Slides (for lessons notes, points, or promotions)
- Email Header
- Facebook | Instagram | Twitter Images

TO SEE THE ENTIRE SERIES, VISIT GROUP.COM/QUICKPICKS